To John

Toilet Paper
Crisis

Wipe away those fears.

Johnny Welsh

Here's a
John Book

Dedicated to all the assholes we know and care so deeply about.

Johnny Welsh

CONTENTS

ACKNOWLEDGMENTS

Special thanks to the lady that made me panic as she bolted out of the store with a thirty-pack of Charmin.

1 NO SHIT

This book is for pure entertainment intended to create a little potty humor in desperate times. Yes, it will be juvenile and silly, but it may make you smile. Downright gross would be another way to describe what you are about to read.

It is not factual and should not be taken as medical or practical advice. The whole book is a joke. Although, you may find a useful idea. The best advice which goes hand in hand (pun intended) with this is to wash your hands; especially after the bathroom. Weren't we supposed to be taught that somewhere in life? Oh, and stay calm for crying out loud!

So, if you are okay with this disclaimer and want to know how to beat a toilet paper shortage/crisis. This book is for you. It is a no-shit approach to ass-wiping in a global pandemic. Consider this your coronavirus survival guide to toilet paper shortage. There is a special offer at the end of this book.

I witnessed a woman running out of Wal-Mart during March of 2020, the coronavirus year, with one of those thirty packs of toilet paper. Is it okay if I say a plus, plus sized woman running? I mean, just for descriptive purposes. To give you a visual, just picture Chris Farley in his lunch lady costume complete with short curly wig and glasses. This is what I see as I am pulling into the parking lot. You can imagine my fear. I mean, if *she's* running... That made me panic a little. Should I run in and grab more TP? Then I began to think and when that happens, my mind wanders off on silly tangents.

I decided it was time to fight the panic with humor. Humor about the toilet paper crisis, not the actual pandemic.

It was true, I went inside and saw an entire aisle empty of supplies. I never thought I'd see the day where we, as human beings, would engage in such selfish behavior. Anyway, back to the humor. You don't need six months' worth of toilet paper and this book will show you why. There are so many fun alternatives to taking care of our high maintenance bottoms.

When did all this ass wiping start? Did cavemen wipe their asses? I did a little research into the topic and discovered that prehistoric people did. You may have thought that the term Stone Age was for other reasons, but the real reason is because they used stones for anal hygiene. One can only imagine why they decided to use the stone in the first place. Was it a burning desire? Animals of many other species just push, drop, and go but humans had a desire to wipe or swipe it out. That's right, prior to the stones, it may have just been a finger or two then wipe that on the cave wall. Talk about leaving your mark in this world.

And we thought they were cave drawings.

Fast forward a million years or so to the Greeks and Romans and it was found that the Greeks used stones as well as pieces of ceramic.

Can you imagine a shard of ceramic in those sensitive areas? Cringe.

So, there was an attempt to advance by using the first of man-made toiletries. The Romans would take this a step further with a sponge-on-a-stick invention that they cleaned off in salty water with vinegar between sessions. This may be where the modern back scrub brush came from. I guess it came in handy for many hard to reach areas.

Let's trek over to Asia and another hundred years later. The same type of shit-stick was found along the Silk Road in the community bathrooms. That means that it was a shared sponge on a stick. Ewww!

What about America? The Colonial days must have made some type of advancement. Can you guess what it might have been? Think Thanksgiving. That's right, corn husks and corn cobs along with animal furs, sticks, leaves, etc. I would prefer a freshly eaten cob over an old dried out one. Just personal preference.

I wonder if an epidemic would have the colonials

scrambling to horde piles of used corn cobs.

THE RABBIT AND THE BEAR

A bear and a rabbit are side by side in the woods taking a shit. The bear looks over at the rabbit and asks, "Hey rabbit, do you ever have any issues with shit sticking to your fur?"

"No, why?" the little rabbit replies.

So, the bear grabs the rabbit in his giant claw and wipes his ass with the little fella'.

Next up from the annals of history would be newspapers, magazines, and books. Those items were very useful as they served two purposes; nourish the mind and then apply to the back end. There's a practical surprise in the back of the paperback version of this book.

Around the late 1700's toilet tissue paper began to come around. It was easy to convince people to buy a softer alternative to newspapers and magazines especially with advertising phrases like, "Splinter-free". I don't even want to think about why that phrase was needed!

Europe didn't see much of this since they had bidets. There were no stories of toilet paper hording coming from European countries throughout our Toilet Paper Crisis.

.

2 MONTHLY USAGE METHOD

We'll start off with how to set yourself up for success for future events such as this current crisis. This will also come in handy should you decide to create a par level or pars for toiletries. The par system is a method for calculating how much of a product you use per week or month that will allow you to stock up for the appropriate time frame. This way, you won't run out and you won't overstock and have money sitting on the shelves. I learned this trick working at bars and restaurants.

This will be vital information, so you know how much toilet paper to purchase in the future to ensure society has enough and no single asshole is left behind. We love our assholes, but we don't need to spoil them in desperate times.

You don't want to be seen sprinting from a store with an armload of more than you could possibly use. Especially, not at your most unfit moment in life.

Monitor your overall usage for a three-month period. It all starts with a little study. A study of you and your family's bathroom habits. I won't lie, it's not very sexy, but it will help you gauge your asshole's needs and the need of other assholes. Set up a notepad and paper near the toilet paper holder or dispenser. No, it's not to wipe your ass with; it's to keep a tally on how many rolls you go through over the course of three months. Next, divide that number by three and you will have your monthly usage needs.

That way, when there is a crisis, you will know exactly how much to buy for you and your family per month. It is important to use the same brand for consistency. Not all rolls are created equal.

You can be even more efficient by ordering online if you must. Check the sites from which you might purchase toilet paper, write down how long it takes for fulfilling the order and shipping. Now, you have more weapons in your asshole arsenal!

3 REUSABLE BABY DIAPERS

Use reusable baby diapers made of cloth and wash them. There are families that do this on a regular basis in order to reduce their costs and carbon footprint. It is possible and not that nasty. The fabric used for these cloths tends to be a bit softer for that nice touch. You gotta keep these assholes happy. If it grosses you out that much, keep a bucket of bleach mixed with water outside as a holding tank. Then toss them in the washer.

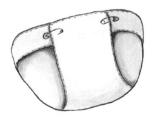

4 CONSERVATIVE FOLD METHOD

Fold-it-up method for maximum 'wipeage' on minimum supplies. There is an amazing way to conserve toilet paper by folding the squares. I think four squares are sufficient for a normal movement. Feel free to use more if you are one of those explosive characters.

Pull off four squares and then fold it in half. Then fold it in half again. You will have a four-ply thick square of about four inches by four inches. That's your biggest swipe. Reach under or around and wipe away. Then, fold that directly in half so the dirty skid mark is folded inside, and your hands are protected. Wipe again. Be sure to keep your fingers on the inside of the tissue paper and not over the edge where you will be saying, "Ewwww!" if you're not careful.

Then take that if it's still in good enough shape and fold it one last time for a little tiny wipe. And, drop. There, you just had three good wipes with only four squares of toilet paper. Repeat until the paper returns with no skid marks. Got it?

My friend, Jamie, told me of a Grand Canyon rafting trip where they have poop talks every night explaining how they need to conserve. There was a two square to swipe wipe one time!

She joked we might need to trade food for toilet paper towards in today's world.

Their motto was do not waste a square out here!

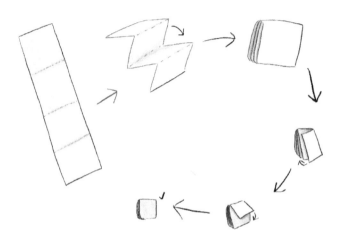

Beware

If a stray random spot shows up
on the outside of the wipe
zone. Don't be confused as to
how it got there; you have a
breach. If this happens, skip to
chapter 7 and hop in the
shower.

BREACH

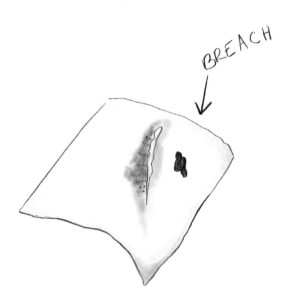

Clean Getaway

This rare and elusive anomaly happens when you check the TP after the reconnaissance wipe and it's already clear. This means you're done. Do not waste any more, done deal. It's time to get away.

Clean getaway. Not to be confused with a ghost poop. That's when you look back in the toilet and there is nothing floating, swimming, or lurking. It can be called The Phantom as well.

5 WHERE'S MY SOCKS?

Start searching for items that you would have thrown away; socks with holes, underwear, old shirts. That's right cut that ratty old t-shirt up into ten pieces and go to town. Worst case scenario, you could go to the local thrift store and buy about ten t-shirts for ten dollars. That's 100 wipes!!! Wooo Hooo!!!

Johnny Welsh

6 TP ALTERNATIVES

Paper towel holder. Install a paper towel holder and use paper towels in a crunch.

Dinner napkin dispenser. Place one of those nice decorative dinner napkin holders that you use on special occasions like Thanksgiving. Fill it with the holiday napkins and there you go.

Neosporin ointment. Keep a supply of Neosporin ointment, Preparation H, or Aquaphor in case of chaffing from the two above. They can be a bit abrasive.

Use leaves in warmer climates. In extreme cases, you could always use leaves. Just be sure to get a book on how to identify leaves so you

don't go wiping your ass with poison ivy.
Believe me, that's a mistake you will only make
once in your life.

Save the cotton from your vitamins. You
know that cotton that you pull out of vitamins
and some medicines? Why not grab some of
that and use it. It may not last long, but it
could save you in a crisis moment when all else
is lost.

Box of tissues coupled with the fold
method. Regular tissues could be used if you
run out. Combine this method with the fold
method in chapter 4.

For extra thin stools, just dab it. I always
wanted to have a website called Dabit.com that
would deal with fun stories like these that
should have been kept private.

For my friends in the Midwest. I would be

remiss if I didn't include some of your old school tried and true methods; corn cobs and corn husks. The husks are self-explanatory, but the cob should be used lengthwise, not perpendicular. This is not that kind of book!

Dryer lint. This one is possible but might need to be coupled with chapter 7, hop in the shower afterwards.

Do not use alcohol wipes. It may be tempting to get a good clean and sterilize while you are at it. Do not be tempted. This is a burn that will have you running to the kitchen sink for the sprayer mentioned earlier.

Don't even think of using Q-Tips. Talk about dabbing it. That's like a pointillism painting. It will take a long while.

"Do you know the difference between toilet paper and a shower curtain?"

"So, you're the one!"

Johnny Welsh

7 WASH THAT ASS OUT

If your toilet is located next to your shower, well, there's an option. If for some apocalyptic reason all the toilet paper is unavailable. Chances are your shower is right next to your toilet. What about hopping in the shower and washing your ass out with a soapy washcloth?

Downward dog in the shower.

This is one of the most famous or common yoga poses. First, disrobe yourself. Then adjust water temperature and get in the shower with the shower on. Face away from the shower faucet and bend over to place your hands about three or four feet in front of you with your ass in the air. Adjust your hips so the stream of water hits in the spot that needs cleaning. Of course, you know this one is a total joke. So, don't try this at home and blame me when you fall. I told you not to do it.

8 BUY OR MAKE A BIDET

Make a homemade bidet with a piece of a rubber glove and an aquarium hose or section of garden hose. Turn the water on gently so as not to winkle yourself. You can find plastic tubing at Lowes, Home Depot, and even a pet store. I would recommend a maximum diameter of a half-inch. Then get some duct tape and a small, thick rubber glove and cut the fingers off the glove and tape the palm tube to the tube. Then, if the glove is tight enough you can stretch it over your tub faucet and turn on the water gently. I would also recommend lukewarm water so as not to shock your ass. Use a towel or paper towel to dry yourself.

Here's one more; use that dish sprayer that nobody else uses anymore in the kitchen sink but only when nobody is home. You may need a stool or chair to stand on. Make sure your ass is over the sink, so you don't spray unmentionables on the floor. Again, check to make sure the water isn't too cold or too hot. Lukewarm feels the best. Then spray away. Of course, you will have to do the wide-legged poop walk so it doesn't smear before you spray. Don't forget to dry.

There are even products that you can purchase that convert your toilet into a bidet. Look up bidets online and you will find a full assortment of them. Battery operated travel bidets are available for a little refresher on the road.

9 MISCELLANEOUS SQUIRTERS

Squirt bottle. A squirt bottle can be used much like a bidet if you can fit it under your ass in the toilet bay area. Make sure your aim is good and begin to squirt. You may use the stream or spray depending on your stool.

Old large syringe. My dad used to bring home giant syringes without the needles, of course. We would play with these as children during bath time. You could fill up a large one of these and use it much like the squirt bottle method.

Turkey baster. You might not want to reuse the baster for turkey dinner after this, but it may work. Your dinner guest may exclaim," This turkey tastes like shit!" As with all the water methods, be sure to dry with a towel or paper towel.

10 THE GLOVE AND THE SQUARE

Rubber gloves with one square.
This was an old joke back in the day. How do you wipe your ass with only one square of toilet paper left? Answer: poke your finger through the middle of the square, clean your ass with your finger. Then use the one square to clean your finger by pulling it up and back over to remove the finger from the hole. The hole of the square, that is. The joke is nasty so that's why I titled this section with a rubber glove in it. That means use a rubber glove to perform this feat, and while we're at it, use two fingers!

~I got in touch with my inner self today, it's the last time I use 1 ply toilet roll~

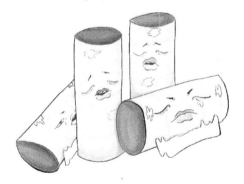

Johnny Welsh

EP-POO-LOGUE

Finally, you can use this book. The last twenty pages are left intentionally blank with an ass wiping target printed for shits and giggles!

It takes a nation of human compassion not to buy up six months' worth of toilet paper in times of a crisis. It is not very altruistic to think only of yourself and your immediate loved ones and horde more than is necessary because the media and news made you panic. Wash your hands and stay calm is a metaphor for chill the fuck out. We will survive this as humans and then continue to live side by side as humans. It's not 'screw your neighbor' so that your asshole has its luxurious treatment every time you poop.

I'm not above any of this as I am an asshole, too. I hope you smiled!

Johnny Welsh

> YES, PLEASE SEND
> ME A STICKER.
> MY ASS
> SURVIVED THE
> COVID CRISIS
> (CUT THIS
> COUPON OUT
> AND SEND IT IN)

There is a special offer after you have read this whole silly book. If you send me an old-fashioned letter with a self-addressed stamped envelope, I will send you your very own, "My ass survived the CoVid crisis" sticker.

Wow, I haven't responded to a mail in offer like this since the '80's, I think. I'm bringing it back. It's so much fun!

Johnny Welsh
Po Box 2046
Frisco, Co 80443

Johnny Welsh

ABOUT THE AUTHOR

Johnny Welsh has worked as a professional bartender in Frisco, Colorado, for over twenty years. He did so well at Syracuse University that they kept him an extra year. After five years of university study, he earned a degree in Italian Language, Literature, and Culture which has been a great prerequisite for a lifelong career in the mixology arts. He can now dictate funny bar stories in two different languages. His latest hobby is twisting these topics into books.

He is the author of Paper Maps, No Apps: An Unplugged Travel Adventure. His first book, Weedgalized in Colorado, about the legalization of marijuana in Colorado, won two awards from Readers' Favorite. Find more at www.JohnnyWelsh.com

ABOUT THE ILLUSTRATOR

Marissa Cristini is a self-taught illustrator. She has only come this far because of the amazing people in her life. Shout to Mr. Cifuni.

Johnny Welsh

This page left blank intentionally

>>>>>>WIPE ZONE<<<<<<<<

This page left blank intentionally

>>>>>>WIPE ZONE<<<<<<<<

This page left blank intentionally

>>>>>>WIPE ZONE<<<<<<<<

This page left blank intentionally

>>>>>>WIPE ZONE<<<<<<<<

This page left blank intentionally

>>>>>>WIPE ZONE<<<<<<<<

This page left blank intentionally

>>>>>>WIPE ZONE<<<<<<<<

This page left blank intentionally

>>>>>>WIPE ZONE<<<<<<<<

This page left blank intentionally

>>>>>>WIPE ZONE<<<<<<<<

This page left blank intentionally

>>>>>>WIPE ZONE<<<<<<<<

This page left blank intentionally

>>>>>>WIPE ZONE<<<<<<<<

This page left blank intentionally

>>>>>>WIPE ZONE<<<<<<<<

This page left blank intentionally

>>>>>>WIPE ZONE<<<<<<<

This page left blank intentionally

>>>>>>WIPE ZONE<<<<<<<<

This page left blank intentionally

>>>>>>WIPE ZONE<<<<<<<<

This page left blank intentionally

>>>>>>WIPE ZONE<<<<<<<<

This page left blank intentionally

>>>>>>WIPE ZONE<<<<<<<<

Made in the USA
Monee, IL
14 April 2020

25853112R00046